D1123505

Snap books™

Queens and Princesses

PRINCESS

Kiko

OF JAPAN

by Tim O'Shei

Capstone
press®

Mankato, Minnesota

Snap Books are published by Capstone Press,
151 Good Counsel Drive, P.O. Box 669, Mankato, Minnesota 56002.
www.capstonepress.com

Library of Congress Cataloging-in-Publication Data
O'Shei, Tim.
   Princess Kiko of Japan / by Tim O'Shei.
   p. cm. — (Snap books. Queens and princesses)
   Includes bibliographical references and index.
   Summary: "Describes the life of Princess Kiko of Japan" — Provided by publisher.
   ISBN-13: 978-1-4296-1958-5 (hardcover)
   ISBN-10: 1-4296-1958-9 (hardcover)
   1. Kiko, Princess of Japan, 1966– — Juvenile literature. 2. Princesses — Japan
— Biography — Juvenile literature. 3. Akishino no Miya Fumihito, Prince, son of
Akihito, Emperor of Japan, 1965– — Juvenile literature. I. Title. II. Series.
DS891.42.K55A3 2009
952.04'9092 — dc22   2008007542

Editor: Angie Kaelberer
Designer: Juliette Peters
Photo Researcher: Wanda Winch

Photo Credits: AP Images/Gregory Bull, 20; AP Images/Imperial Household
Agency, HO, 28 (right); AP Images/Imperial Palace, 23; AP Images/Koji Sasahara,
13, 25; Corbis/Sygma, 19; Getty Images Inc./AFP, 28 (left); Getty Images Inc./AFP/J.
Kurokawa, 12; Getty Images Inc./Itsuo Inouye, 26; Getty Images Inc./Junko Kimura,
cover; Getty Images Inc./Koichi Kamoshida, 9; The Image Works/Fujifotos, 6, 15, 16,
29; Kyodo News, 10; Landov LLC/Kyodo, 5

Capstone Press thanks Fred G. Notehelfer, PhD, Professor of History and former
director of the Terasaki Center for Japanese Studies, University of California, Los
Angeles, for his assistance with this book.

Essential content terms are **bold** and are defined at the bottom of the page where
they first appear.

1 2 3 4 5 6 13 12 11 10 09 08

Table of Contents

A Life-Changing DAY

Kiko Kawashima opened her eyes, swung her feet to the floor, and stepped out of bed. Today was a very important day in her life.

At 4:30 in the morning, the Tokyo sky was dark. Most of Japan was sound asleep. But in just a few hours, millions across Japan and around the world would be watching a grand event. Kiko was the star, and it was time to get ready.

In 1985, Kiko Kawashima (second from right) met her future husband (right) at college.

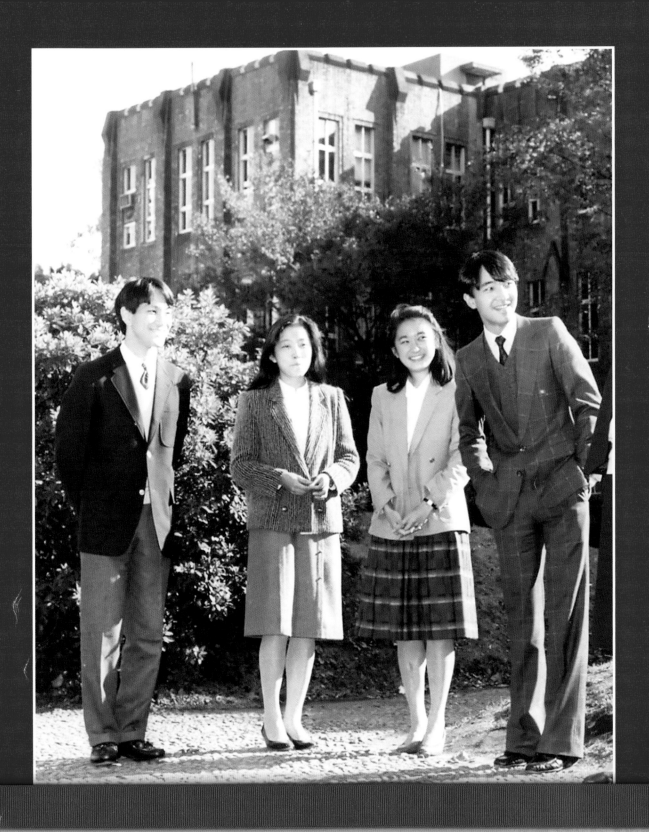

Kiko and her parents (right) met with a palace official to plan her wedding.

AN UNCOMMON DAY

The date was June 29, 1990. When it began, 23-year-old Kiko was a **commoner**. She was an intelligent young woman from an ordinary family. She lived in an apartment with her parents and her 16-year-old brother, Shu.

In college, Kiko dated a student named Fumihito, whose nickname was Aya. They fell in love and decided to get married. Unlike Kiko, Aya wasn't a commoner. He was the son of Japanese Emperor Akihito. In just a few hours, Kiko would marry Aya and become a princess.

Two hours after Kiko awoke, a limousine arrived outside her parents' apartment building. Kiko's family walked her outside. She bowed deeply to her family as they said good-bye. The next time Kiko saw her family, she would no longer be simply Kiko. She would be Princess Kiko of Japan.

"I saw him (the prince) talking to his friends, and I thought he was much more unpretentious than I expected."
—Princess Kiko on her first meeting with Prince Fumihito

2

A WORLDLY Childhood

Kiko was born in Tokyo, Japan, on September 11, 1966. Her parents are Tatsuhiko and Kazuyo Kawashima. Kiko's father is a college professor. His specialty is economics, which is the study of how goods and services are produced and used.

When Kiko was a little girl, her family moved to the United States. Kiko's father wanted to earn a doctorate, which is the highest college degree a person can receive. Tatsuhiko studied for his doctoral degree at the University of Pennsylvania in Philadelphia. He also taught classes there.

The Kawashima family spent six years in Philadelphia. Kiko learned a lot about American culture and language. She still speaks English well today. When Kiko was in elementary school, her family moved to Vienna, Austria. Kiko lived there into her teens and learned to speak German well. Her knowledge of languages and cultures would one day help Kiko represent Japan.

Tokyo Tower is a well-known landmark in the city where Kiko was born.

When they were dating, Aya and Kiko enjoyed skiing and other outdoor activities.

MEETING THE PRINCE

Kiko attended college back in Japan. She studied psychology at Gakushuin University. As a freshman, she joined a nature club. The club's leader, Aya, was one year older than Kiko.

Kiko liked Aya, who was studying **zoology**. But she treated him with the respect usually given to someone much older. She had good reasons. Aya was Emperor Hirohito's grandson. One day, Aya's father would be emperor. So Kiko didn't call him "Aya," or even "Prince." When she first met her future husband, Kiko called him "Your Imperial Highness."

Aya was charmed. Kiko was polite, soft-spoken, and a good listener. Kiko and Aya started to spend more time together and quickly grew close. Before long, they were in love.

One day, Kiko and Aya were walking to Kiko's house from the university. They stopped at a traffic light. Aya asked Kiko, "Will you spend your life with me?" She said yes.

Kiko and Aya announced their wedding plans in September 1989. Emperor Hirohito had died earlier that year. Aya's father, Akihito, was now emperor.

The wedding was big news in Japan. Aya would be the first of the new emperor's children to get married. Aya's older brother, Naruhito, was still single. So was his younger sister, Sayako. Aya's marriage meant the emperor might have grandchildren. If one of them was a boy, he could become emperor of Japan one day.

JAPAN MEETS KIKO

Interest in Kiko swept Japan. The last commoner to marry into the imperial family was the empress, Michiko. She married Akihito in 1959. Because Aya wasn't the crown prince, Kiko was unlikely to ever be empress. But even as a princess, she would be an important role model for Japanese girls and women.

The Japanese people liked Kiko. She was shy, polite, smart, and pretty. In Japanese culture, those qualities are considered important in women. Sometimes people called her Kiko-chan, which means "little Kiko." Her gentle smile became known as the "Kiko smile."

Kiko (right) was the first commoner to marry into the imperial family since Empress Michiko (second from left).

JAPAN'S IMPERIAL SUCCESSION

"Succession" is the word that describes who will become emperor next. In Japan, women aren't part of the line of succession. Only men can take the throne and become emperor.

When Emperor Akihito dies, his oldest son, Naruhito, stands next in line to become emperor. That's why Naruhito's full title is Crown Prince Naruhito. If Naruhito died or for some reason couldn't become emperor, Kiko's husband would become emperor.

Seems simple, right? It is, but only if boys are born. For more than 40 years, that didn't happen. The situation caused the Japanese people much stress.

BECOMING A

Princess

On her wedding day, Kiko wore a silk **kimono** that belonged to the royal family. It was worth about $230,000. An ordinary bride could buy about 300 wedding dresses for that much money! Putting on the 35-pound (16-kilogram) kimono took two hours. It had 12 layers and many colors. Kiko's black hair was arranged in a smooth bun. A large golden comb held the bun in place.

Prince Aya's wedding clothes were simpler. He wore a black headdress and a black robe. Underneath the robe, he wore a red garment decorated with cranes flying among the clouds. The crane is a symbol of long life and good luck.

Kiko's wedding kimono had 12 colorful layers of silk.

kimono — a long, loose robe with wide sleeves and a sash

IMPORTANT GUESTS

The wedding took place at a **shrine** inside the Imperial Palace grounds. Kiko's family was there. So were Crown Prince Naruhito, Princess Sayako, Japan's prime minister, and 150 other guests.

Two very important people were not there, however. Emperor Akihito and Empress Michiko stayed away. In Japanese tradition, the emperor and empress don't attend their children's weddings. The emperor receives a lot of attention. His presence would have taken the focus away from Kiko and Aya. Instead, Akihito and Michiko watched the wedding on TV, along with 98 million other Japanese.

Aya and Kiko were married at the Kashikodokoro Shrine.

shrine — a place used for Japanese religious celebrations

They didn't have to watch long, though. The entire ceremony took only 11 minutes. The prince walked down an aisle to the altar. Kiko walked a few steps behind him. They bowed twice at the altar. Aya read a traditional wedding prayer, "We pledge to love each other and to cherish each other. This will not change, forever." The couple then sipped a rice wine called sake.

After the ceremony, the prince and his new princess visited his parents. The emperor and empress held a private celebration for the newlyweds. Akihito then gave the couple the new names of Prince and Princess Akishino. Still, the Japanese people would call their princess by a simpler name — Kiko.

A SPECIAL RING

Kiko's engagement ring was made just for her. The ring is in the shape of two catfish twisted together. In college, Prince Akishino spent much of his time studying catfish.

AN *Imperial* LIFE

After the wedding, Kiko and Akishino climbed into a limousine. About 30,000 people lined the Tokyo streets to greet the newlyweds. About 9,000 police officers were on hand to control the crowd. The couple took a six-minute ride to their new home. It was a one-story house on the palace grounds. People cheered as Kiko smiled and waved to them.

Kiko had changed into a sleeveless white gown and a diamond necklace and bracelet. On her head was a tiara covered with 3,000 diamonds.

The crowd watched Princess Kiko closely. Little girls gazed at her jewelry. Women gasped, "Oh, she's so beautiful!"

After the wedding, Kiko wore a shimmering white gown to greet the Japanese public.

Kiko greeted children during a visit to Mexico in 1997.

A PRINCESS' JOB

Japan's imperial family doesn't run the country. The people elect a prime minister and parliament to do that. But the emperor's family does represent the country. Prince Akishino and Princess Kiko have represented Japan in countries all over the world.

At home, Princess Kiko is involved in the Red Cross and other health organizations. She supports education and has translated children's books from English into Japanese. After her marriage, Kiko continued her own education. In 1995, she received a master's degree in psychology.

During college, Kiko learned sign language. Each year, she attends a sign language contest for high school students. Kiko has even given speeches in sign language.

IMPERIAL HOUSEHOLD AGENCY

Japan's imperial family is one of the most mysterious families in the world. The Imperial Household Agency (IHA) wants it that way.

This government agency has about 1,000 employees. They do everything from cleaning the family's homes to preparing the tombs when a family member dies.

The IHA's leader is the Grand Steward. He and his assistants run most areas of the imperial family's lives. The IHA has to approve the trips family members take and the organizations they support. The IHA also controls who speaks to the family. If the prime minister wants to talk to the emperor, he asks the IHA first.

The IHA keeps secret most details of imperial life. Little information is known about Kiko's hobbies, opinions, or dreams. The IHA doesn't like the emperor's family to show emotion in public. At Kiko's wedding, a photographer took a photo of her smoothing Akishino's hair. The IHA thought the photo was too personal. The agency tried to stop magazines and newspapers from printing it.

Do the family members ever get tired of the IHA's tight grip? Probably so, but most of them won't say so.

WHO WILL TAKE THE THRONE?

Early in 1991, Akishino and Kiko learned they were going to have a baby. Princess Mako was born in October 1991. Princess Kako followed in December 1994. Meanwhile, Crown Prince Naruhito married. He and his wife, Masako, also had a daughter. This created a major problem in Japan. None of the girls could take the throne. According to the current Imperial Household Laws, only a prince can become emperor.

The Japanese people were worried. Politicians were worried. Some reports claimed that even the emperor was worried. Japan's parliament considered changing the laws to allow a princess to take the throne.

Then, in early 2006, the Japanese people learned some exciting news. Princess Kiko was pregnant! Members of parliament broke into applause. They quickly decided not to change the law — for now. But one big question remained: Would the baby be a boy?

Akishino and Kiko have two daughters, Mako (lower left) and Kako (lower right).

THE Wait IS Over

During her pregnancy, the Japanese people watched Princess Kiko even more closely than before. If she were to have a boy, he could be the future emperor of Japan. But if the baby was a girl, the debate over succession would continue.

The Japanese people prayed for a safe pregnancy and delivery. So did the prince and princess. One month before the baby was due, Kiko took part in a prayer ceremony. She wore an ivory silk dress. An assistant helped wrap her in a red-and-white sash. Prince Akishino tied the knot. Together, they said prayers. The ceremony was held on the Asian Day of the Dog. Dogs are believed to have an especially easy time giving birth.

Princess Kiko attended a meeting of Japan's Red Cross three months before her baby was due.

COMPLICATIONS

Much of the concern over Princess Kiko's pregnancy was caused by her age. She was 39, which made complications more likely. Unfortunately, that's what happened. In August 2006, Kiko was diagnosed with placenta previa. The placenta, which connects the baby to the mother's uterus, dropped too low. Kiko entered the hospital on August 16. Her husband, daughters, and even the emperor and empress visited and kept her company.

Mako filled her mom in on a recent visit with family friends in Austria. She shared some of the CDs she bought there. Kako visited her mother nearly every day. She did her homework at the side of Kiko's bed and told her what was going on at home.

The prince and princess were overjoyed by their son's birth.

IT'S A BOY!

On the morning of September 6, 2006, Kiko's wait was over. The baby was born — and it was a boy!

Throughout Japan, TV stations cut in on their regular programming to share the big news. The new prince was healthy, and Kiko was doing well too. At a glance, the prince was a normal, 5-pound, 10-ounce (2.6-kilogram) baby. But everyone knew this baby was special. One day, he could be the emperor of Japan.

It took another week for the Imperial Household Agency to pick the baby's name. It is Hisahito, which means virtuous, calm, and everlasting. The IHA said it chose the name with the wish that the new prince has a long life, a good temper, and peace of mind.

IMPERIAL KIDS

Young members of the imperial family learn early about their future responsibilities. Like their parents, they get royal titles. Kiko's daughters are formally called "Her Imperial Highness Princess Mako" and "Her Imperial Highness Princess Kako." Even little Hisahito is called "His Imperial Highness."

But aside from that, they're normal kids. Princess Kako, who was 11 when her brother was born, likes figure skating and crafts. While her mom was pregnant, she made felt toys for the baby.

Princess Mako was 14 when Prince Hisahito was born. She enjoys art, listening to music, and playing the piano. In 2006, she made her first trip alone when she visited friends in Austria.

LIFE TODAY

Princess Kiko's life revolves around her family. Her daughters turn to her for advice on dealing with school, friends, and other teenage concerns. She's also raising her son to be the next emperor of Japan. It's a big job, but the calm, confident princess is up to the challenge.

Today, Kiko focuses on raising Kako, Hisahito, and Mako to represent Japan one day.

Glossary

commoner (KAH-muh-nuhr) — a person who isn't part of a royal or imperial family

doctorate (DAHK-tuh-ruht) — the highest degree a person can earn from a college or university

economics (EK-uh-NOM-iks) — the study of the production and use of goods and services

imperial (im-PIHR-ee-uhl) — in Japan, anything related to the emperor or his family

kimono (kuh-MOH-noh) — a long, loose robe with wide sleeves and a sash

parliament (PAR-luh-muhnt) — an elected group of the people's representatives who make laws for a country

placenta previa (pluh-SEN-tuh PREH-vee-uh) — a condition that occurs when the tissue that attaches a baby to its mother's uterus drops too low

prime minister (PRIME MIN-uh-stur) — the elected head of Japan's government

shrine (SHRINE) — a place used for Japanese religious celebrations

zoology (zoh-OL-uh-jee) — the science of studying animals

Read More

Burgan, Michael. *Japan.* Questions and Answers Countries. Mankato, Minn.: Capstone Press, 2005.

Messager, Alexandre. *We Live in Japan.* Kids Around the World. New York: Abrams Books, 2007.

Reynolds, Jeff. *Japan.* A to Z. New York: Children's Press, 2004.

Streissguth, Thomas. *Japan.* Country Explorers. Minneapolis: Lerner, 2008.

Internet Sites

FactHound offers a safe, fun way to find Internet sites related to this book. All of the sites on FactHound have been researched by our staff.

Here's how:

1. Visit **www.facthound.com**
2. Choose your grade level.
3. Type in this book ID **1429619589** for age-appropriate sites. You may also browse subjects by clicking on letters, or by clicking on pictures and words.
4. Click on the **Fetch It** button.

FactHound will fetch the best sites for you!

Index